ABOUT THE AUTHOR

Dide is an award-winning multi-disciplinary writer, artist and composer-performer. In 2023 she became a Royal Society of British Artists' Rising Star. *Making Sense* is her debut poetry collection. Her debut poetry pamphlet, *Growing*, was published in 2022.

Website: www.dide.uk
Instagram: @_d_i_d_e_

'You don't recognise what's new until you trip over it. So many poems are busily trying to sound like whatever trend is just about to be over, but these poems seem to come out of nowhere. Strange they are, in the ways they use metaphor, in the ways they remake the world; but most of what they are is true, brave and touching. I didn't see them coming.'
- **Mark Waldron**

'Throughout this gorgeous debut collection, Dide's unique ability to create images that startle, shock and surprise enthrals – they will make you look at the world afresh. She says it best herself: "any minute of any hour, you make me put eyes in my eyes".'
- **Rishi Dastidar**

'An unflinching and unique body of work sharing perspectives on Borderline Personality Disorder and Autism and what it is for a female to be othered in a world of neuro-uniformity. Dide's voice is cool and exacting in the articulation of society's double standards, in calling out power structures, how othering is a methodology of control and how early life experiences are carelessly overlooked within the labelling/categorising of human behavioural tendencies. Despite being political in this way, the collection is deeply personal and often shocking in candour and philosophical eloquence: "cortisol and testosterone helped annihilate whole cities". Language is lifted out of tropes and refreshed to the point where synaesthesia (as reported by the narrator) becomes actualised. A subtle seam of homage to the arts and music as a form of nurture runs through the work providing further expansion of discourse. Whilst this debut is serious at core, a skilled playfulness with form and curiosity makes it wholly compelling, allowing the reader to come away buoyant and altered, paying closer attention to the world: "some ailments radiate an unusual heat, others an ache, others a stab, and others still, pressure of a still day".'
- **Rushika Wick**

DIDE
Making Sense

VERVE
POETRY PRESS
BIRMINGHAM

PUBLISHED BY VERVE POETRY PRESS
https://vervepoetrypress.com
mail@vervepoetrypress.com

All rights reserved
© 2023 Dide

The right of Dide to be identified as author of this work has been asserted in accordance with section 77 of the Copyright, Designs and Patents Act 1988.

No part of this work may be reproduced, stored or transmitted in any form or by any means, graphic, electronic, recorded or mechanical, without the prior written permission of the publisher.

FIRST PUBLISHED APR 2023

Printed and bound in the UK
by ImprintDigital, Exeter

ISBN: 978-1-913917-35-7

Cover image, copyright Dide, 'Bruise on the thigh', oil on canvas

For continuance – the continued effort of knowledge, betterment, acceptance, recycled matter and possible existence

Dedicated to my Mother and Father

CONTENTS

Parkour	11
O	12
Homage	13
Levels 1 to 4 in 10 minutes	14
a) before I knew what poems could be, I wrote 'little texts',	15
A Cubist take on a moment in time	16
An uncertain time	17
Stalker	18
Aftermath	19
The event	20
Advertising	21
b) 'In the commune' marketed version	22
Aunt	23
How to describe pain	24
A manual for those with mild autism	25
Psalm 31.7	26
When cortisol rises,	27
like a line of cocaine, the sex-drug creating	28
Psalm 43	29
Time and...	30
c) "We are not emotional seesaws.	31
Sorry fakery	32
Russian doll	33

Two for the price of one	34
Sisyphus' PMDD	35
In the pub quiz	36
, and	37
Bread and chocolate	38
Palestine	39
d) ideas on 'little text'	40
Lies	41
Through thick and thin	42
The hammam	43
Playing Sims	44
The stages of childbirth	45
Crossing the border	47
e) Shutup,	48
The Acclaimed	49
A polyptych of experts	50
Tinnitus/ˈtɪnɪtəs/noun, MEDICINE	52
Second life	53
The exoskeleton of the partially deaf	54
Rush hour	55
f) little philosophy text	56
In a world where you can be anything,	57
It's not true that	58
Things like asparagus	59
Psalm 15	60
My friend Shane	61

S-s-s-	62
The juncture	63
g) little recipe	65
'Mahl' is the German word for 'meal'	66
Foreplay	67
Note on Shakespeare's "Tired with all these, for restful death I cry"	68
Dearest Beethoven,	69
Little dot	70
Dead fox	71
A part of my body is dead,	72

Annex

---

* *The search for Mol, a footnote poem*

Making Sense

Parkour

How many times,
I have seen that word slip
and tumble to tarmac,

you don't understand.

Missing posters up down every decade, image so wholesome can't help but love Mol, try to find Mol [go to page 23]

O

A chunk in my left abdomen has gone
I walk around like a hagstone on the beach
a postbox
a glory hole for a hand in the shape of
a constant draught   here

it's in the form of your dead eyebrow
which is like my eyebrow
I touch mine to remember yours
when I want a hug, or a word
rarely given before, not through lacked love

my days turn to lead white
I ask myself how long you've been absent
how long the sky has been this vacant grey
I feel it's a trick question
you transformed so quickly into other roles
I care not for .... with their ....
grieve for ease and champagne laughter
while I'm in my house desiring this alone
and you're next door, in yours.

Homage

You are an umbrella or a spade,
the suffragette, the gut feeling,
hindsight that shows direction   you can be
how your knees must buckle

under weight of those you hold:
guilt, shame, sadness   exasperation
who mother-hens you if you do the
looking after? Dear anger, my love,

I feel sorry for you as I do the bully
so convinced so weak, you lost
your childhood make-believing adult,
festered in boilers without embraces,

come out   come down,
let us teach you to eat with knives
and forks, like we once did a
chimp at the dining table.

Levels 1 to 4 in 10 minutes

They should call it seeing blue,
with the speed of a mountain
sunset, and by that, I mean
victorious. It makes things
unpleasantly hot with no breeze.
Most think blue is cool, cold
royal Raynaud's, the baked-Alaska
glow of a snow cave. But anger is
violent blue violet, the hottest
flame for cooking 'n forging, when
truth shoots bloody words and
leaves targets, itself, dribbling.

---

* *Is Mol existence, evolution or improvement, or change, motion or movement? [go to page 67]*

a)   before I knew what poems could be, I wrote 'little texts',

and here is one:

> "My eyes don a different impression to what they really are, like my character. They change like my character, from dehydrated grass to amber, depending on depth of inspection and season, temporal and cloth. I had a friend, whose eyes were nothing spectacular, small and squinty you wouldn't have looked twice, but when you did, you saw Saturn-tinged sunflowers. Another had Riviera eyes, another, ice that melts and re-freezes, melts and re-freezes. One had a striking pair that stole glances away. Another was so close to personal standard it was hard to look (easier to see the scaffold than the full self of character). Eyes, through physicality as much as emotion, give away secrets, often discovered too late."

A Cubist take on a moment in time

It's raining in this corner of my eye,
and it's raining in that corner of my eye,
and all at the same time, I'm
- o thankful for the rubber roof above my head
- o hit by the basicness of my architecture – the lack of development in the premise of shelter
- o hit by the flimsiness, like an empty Malteser's chocolate box
- o soaked in the weight of Claudia Rankine's chapter on Serena Williams, my heart rate spiked with toffee-popcorn injustice
- o sunk by the sky-blue clarity of Rankine's words that push a fleshy finger deeper into the seep of a soft flesh wound
- o mindful of my own discolouration from a possible personal action depriving me of sleep for days, heart rate skipping over each lung like a girl, each side of a rope
- o wary whether my mental state is guiding me to respond in the way hoped to Rankine's offering of a shoe
- o agreeing that the body does have a memory, which only a new different memory can start to break, in love as in politics, in gender as in race, in games of hawk and crow
- o reminded of how my refugee parents asked me to choose an English name
- o reminded of how I had to use this name in white English working class society – swimming competitions, building regulations, vets, doctors, banks, beauty salons – where a kiwi was the most exotic and unusual import
- o reminded how I was told I was not black, white or mixed, suggested to leave matters of race to those truly affected, yet not knowing which form box to tick.

An uncertain time

The butting tree carcass she drove past
looked like a miniature brown bear
the radio talking of the government
instructing on how to make Molotov
Cocktails *,* and then an exposed
silvering branch roared with the spear
of a cat trying to maul the zebra
rear of the vehicle in front as a voice
expressed gratitude at the fortune of
filling petrol the night before it all broke
out *,* and she wondered what animal
would next leap out during accounts of
giving blood and other war preparations
in a far country she had minimal ties to.

Stalker

+ then a murder of messages
all demanding my bone marrow
that recalling amounts to

+ then any minute of any hour, you
make me put eyes in my eyes
to catch you early at the door
to see my z c t q route of escape

+ then initiating:

another marker on my nest

how I park my car at night
carry a reprocessed knife

PC 360703, you control what I wear,
what I feel, were supposed to reassure
and not replicate

the Sagittarius who means less
than my compost bin, held me hostage
to hiding than living like women
growth in their feet, says he's following
and will continue to do.

But which question best describes Mol? [go to page 48]

Aftermath

I see a man's face in a toilet rim
in the pile of cumin on a teaspoon
the light switch car steering wheel
the head of my shadow
apron of the grocery assistant
as I would
     see a fire in my shoe
     in my parrot's ear canal
     inferno out the tap, the mini
     waterfall as useless as swiping
     a fingerful of dust,
if I were you: who said "my life
changed forever" the zeptosecond
the Jenga burnt down.

The event

As her hands pulped
the igloo-shaped egg
for the soft-boiled dog,   a blackeye clot
the size of a split lentil
hung, like   a cut-out belly button.

From that moment on
an egg would never be   an egg

knuckles deep in hot yellow   foetus

like when I was attacked by   a man
in the wild of a foreign hike,
hours from a saviour: an
8-year-old girl with her cow.

Gagging like an inexperienced sucker
on chocolate sauce oozing
the bone china hovering   for a drip

. I've waited five days for this respite

from my mid-week raw-plant diet, lusting
for a force-fed happily-ever-after of taste
better enjoyed in the mind, how corks =
celebration, harm, an alarm + other
seductive blueprints of emotional evidence.

All week I chopped uncooked peppers
and carrots, made rainbows burst
and turned coconuts to milk

waiting for colour to dim, the browns
and buffs of peanut butter, chips,
hummus, my whole body
scratched skinless, still itching, still
easing that naked tongue closer.

b) 'In the commune' marketed version

The language of politics was my bedrock , something that did not govern my days but where adults woodliced after dark, the raucous jollity of which lured me to peer through the crack in the kitchen door and then run back, past the grand in the old carriage-hall, up the stone spiral staircase I fell down once, across the landing where my thumb-suck-toy hung weening himself, over the assault course on the carpet grid I played cars, and breathless into bed, waiting with suppressed adrenaline to see if I had made it, or if I had lured them to peer through the crack in my bedroom door; we carried water to our secret garden in wet skirts; got stuck in quick sands and pulled straight out of wellies by big zaftig men; lost the guinea pig in the hedge maze; we had a swan who terrorised the neighbours; cooked meals for thirty and ate them together, and pretended to be lions; there were tunnels underneath the house that went to the sea and every house in the vicinity; all the moustachioed men watched *The Sound of Music* as that was my favourite musical too, and everything that came out of my mouth was song, even this line; I had all the light – an only child gets from staunch parents, others trying out their parenting skills, and children who visited or whom we saw at weekends, one stayed for three years and was my little sister; the best place for children to grow, in free and weird sanctuary.

Aunt

It seems obvious to me now
that my mouth would've been the cave
and my hair the wood, my ear, rock pools
where kids could've spent all day
combing the same stretch for a new piece
of old stone. The prince always left and
always returned, his travels across my bedtime
face, in vain. He visited all the sights a
child of six imagined, but the two mudflats
and the treacherous cliff of the nose – none
held what he was scouting for. And of course,
like every story in search of an end, upon
trailing once more through the tangle, and
bellowing into the monstrous maw, the hunt
stopped at the start, in his hometown,
where his princess finally stood. And each
made-up story was a piece of magic
that wrapped me to you like prosciutto to
melon. And only now, after my own life has
mimicked your stories, am I realising
the full joy of self-return, that leads to
self-knowledge in a way only depression can
lead to light, that is, if you're lucky enough.

---

* Mol is more than family, but many start there. Mol has often be confused for its twin, Mohl [the meaning of a happy life], that no wonder the answer was happiness or an alternative [go to page 35]

How to describe pain

There's resistance, like slowly pushing a Faber-Castell fibre tip pen back into the irretrievable, a pain that says *don't go further*, I think arthritic fingers, without cucumbers or cress;

there's the red burrowing in the throat that feels like a tunnel that'll time travel to somewhere exciting but is usually just a cold;

the pain that stops you from thinking about it, X-rated till you're old or ready enough like wine and dark chocolate;

the pain of everyday shows its face as doubt or indecision, not the same – you thought the table perfect until the sceptic said its legs were unreal;

heartbreak has its own hysteria that propels you to chase after the flee-er with the instinct of the pack or the automation of the engineered;

then there's the sting that draws you closer until numb, how people hope to be through sexual union, but really, it's just a paper cut's small dog bark;

some ailments radiate an unusual heat, others an ache, others a stab, and others still, pressure of a still day;

the too much of suicidal pain later blocked by the mind, a reflective fireproof blanket;

there's the pain of straining for analysis that eludes like a memory of ourselves, just reactive matter joined in a certain way, like capybara, chives and guinea fowl;

so the question has never been whether to be, but rather how.

A manual for those with mild autism

You smile and nod, to show you're friend;
make little noises of encouragement whilst they speak,
but not so loud that you overshadow; do not broach
topics of fertility, politics, religion, money, Wagner;
best avoid overfamiliarity, unless seeking the meat market;
pressing certain points on your hand, or counting, can help calm,
such as L14 or even HT7 and of course the fingertips, when someone
has lost all mind, staring you down like a cow, in fact, go away –
to the loo, to some tidy order – to think through, precisely,
the algorithm that might be causing their unaccountable behaviour,
return with a game plan, some malleable reason for their conduct
that renders you, alone, in this vacuum of beefy denseness;
be on your own a lot, that way their stupidity
shouldn't overwhelm too much, and find strategies for
when it does, that way, they shouldn't find you out.

Psalm 31.7

Most people don't think tidying is the sexiest thing,
but most people don't straighten their eyebrows
five times, spray room freshener three times,
eat crackers in pairs, and group foods eaten in a day
into numbers easily counted on one hand; as calming
as stroking an arm at the perfect rate of 3 cm/s, as
reassuring as staring at rows of tins in supermarkets
for half an hour, do what comes naturally, even when
the normal try to turn you into a messy thoughtless
heap of desert existence.

When cortisol rises,

I check the house lock five times, then all the plug sockets, a feeding frenzy sharking the kitchen.

When cortisol rises, I Tourette's to five – 1 2 3 4 5 – halfway through – 1 2 3 4 5 – a sentence.

Objects need to be placed at right angles and not sticking out of cupboards when cortisol rises.

A cortisol rise could be good for some things, though nothing comes straight to mind, except maybe a fun level of libido.

Cortisol and testosterone helped annihilate whole cities.

Some say – 1 2 3 4 5 – we're struggling to evolve as fast as society, though natural selection can be seen in a lifetime, or that there are fewer dangers, as they leave their house with a hammer

suicide from the sky, a masturbating man on the corner, toxic positivity, the conveyor belt of more, the ever-closer natural disaster...

No wonder – 1 2 3 – people rely – 4 5 1 – on lucky charms – 2 3 – when changing dangers – 4 5 – add up.

like a line of cocaine, the sex-drug creating

waves was the name of MIND's
Borderline Personality Disorder Programme
I didn't tell

la mère/mer didn't need such information
it came from her and was her
crashing choppy emotions like raw

gems lay on the seabed, ready for capitalist
pirates to exploit, but no matter
it brought silk pillowcases and health
smoothies and finally, stillness to roam free

insulated by the Celotex© of feeling valued –

for so long have other people gaslit water's
misunderstood hydrogen and oxygen
due to their damaged chemic compounds,

my heart is a plastic bag with a cavity in it.

Psalm 43

Flare-ups that toothpaste
nor strip can eliminate,
nothing in the medical cabinet,
and not even the force
of a carpet cleaner. Such
outbreaks of Borderline
make you feel an alcoholic
washing your face in whisky,
a diabetic fed only Percy Pigs,
every minute a multigym
of emotion that kingfishers
into blankness. Nine symptoms
– of which one is uncertainty –
whose reality is far from sitting
on the fence, but leaping
from hot spring to ice
in a way that's not good
for circulation. All things tried or
suggested, such as drinking
shatavari root tea and
tablets from a shaman,
but most importantly,
adopt an un-overwhelming
lifestyle full of rocks and
sharks' teeth and other
grounding elements
when managing, not recovery,
is what's being foraged for.

Time and...

my violin teacher, the great Heifetz's protégé,
said I had a unique relationship with time
and upon reflecting now, it seems Borderline
also gifts such specialness, the goal a dwindling
of hourly mood swings, to daily, to weekly,
quarterly, but not disappearing, and so I pause

on "loss doesn't ease with time" on the page

for the spaces between pangs of grief increase

as other preoccupations scuttle

to the forefront of the mind

long periods of green wifi connectivity

only rarely displaying pained vermillion

and in this way frequency of remembering eases

though the traumaed body

breathes **space** differently.

---

* Sometimes an incomplete phrase makes no sense due to incompleteness, through implication, grows into an entity that demands an answer [go to page 33]

c) **"We are not emotional seesaws.**

> We are not behaviour either, but perhaps in the difficulty that somebody would think the same thoughts in the same order caused by the same thoughts and causing the same thoughts."

You can upscale anything with a designation of a term, and so evolve meaning acute to cute:

> he committed the act due to 'schizophrenia'
> Duchamp said the urinal a fountain
> a paper proclaims you're espoused,

[handwritten: So here's another 'poem': "Identity".]

Sorry fakery

the lubricant unjustly taken for the real,
crying its Imposter Syndrome into pillows,
burdened with the masking task of perfection

Sorry Devil

also unjustly taken for the real   source of evil
yet solitarily genuine and unaware of wrong
while many-shouldered Gods frolic together

Sorry Moon

also taken as the only one, but nameless, with a
definite article while elsewhere badly spoken
siblings unhinge like inarticulate lorries.

Even if we were the only human on an alien
planet, would we rather be called The Human
while billions existed on Earth, or Jemima?

Russian doll

like a hole that's like black

like a Filofax that's like a club sandwich

like a vacuum cleaner that's like a social face

like a mascot like a shield of armour or a lolly

like the smallest integer that's like a woman

like a rug that's like an overlooked legal clause

like a girl that's a cress-control science project

like a mind like another country's nuclear

like a dream like a discarded shopping list

---

* Let's say Mol is evolution. See how the picture changes the more you look at it.

Two for the price of one

There is no Other Sue, the Other Sue is just This Sue, and the surest way of making the Other Sue show their face is to carefully lay adoration at the feet of This Sue, congratulate This Sue on being here with the Other Sue banished, herald This Sue as the True Sue and not mention the unmentionable Other Sue, the Other Sue who machetes thorny thickets trying to free themselves of pinpricks that hurt but leave no visible mark except the obvious clearing

of their rampage.

Sisyphus' PMDD

The hares follow the moles, and after that
the muntjac that nips my Mum's tulip heads,
and then the fallen foliage rises back
with the magnetism of the sun

and while dandruff still clots its branches,
the hunger, excitement, impatience and self-dysmorphia,
in turn wheels round, as heavy as a buzzard, with the
leaves hardly ever just free in the air.

---

* Basic law might see Mol in the good, but not only good people go missing though mostly good people have missing flyers [go to page 41]

In the pub quiz

they showed a zoomed-in map of my country that I didn't get. I covered my embarrassment how women do their bodies in some parts of the world. I guess my mind didn't go there because Anglo-American policy had all been about Greek feta cheese, Arab baklava, Israeli houmous, Uygur meat, Russian salads, Mediterranean platters, Mediterranean mezes, Mediterranean tapas, and everything else, from gözleme to mantı, boiled down to a sugary delight that had nothing to do with lokum and late-night fish & chip shops that sold kebab.

, and

the Oxford comma isn't used in England, which often likes to see itself as Oxford, or Cambridge, with London a completely different cosmopolitan breed, how ironic that our direct water neighbours adopted it, along with place names, I wonder if they felt sorry for it like our street neighbours who adopted those two rescue dogs from Bosnia even though the (Yugoslav) wars had ended long ago, but we know how long it takes to pick yourself up from turmoil of any kind, so all we can do is segment the effort into bitesize bits, small wins, and easily identifiable goals.

Bread and chocolate

Six leathery immigrant men jostle behind metal mesh in a stooped-low chicken hut that leaves backs hunched and plucked white feathers on the walls. Their faces grime clogged, like dirty gold joining of broken Japanese pottery, are pressed on the chicken wire, as they watch an idyllic scene set around a woodland lake of golden Swiss frolicking naked, their starry manes flicking with the horses. The film is called 'Pane e Cioccolata', bread and chocolate, a cheap dessert I ate before I watched the film, hard chocolate body on bouncy yeasty air –

I didn't go to trampolining places or have roller-skates that lit.

So, my father told me to speak English better than most English, which I did. He knew it'd be my *open sesame*, which it was.

I was even adopted into a family that knew the Queen. They were nice to me, but I had cosy nightmares of laughing at the right things and picking up the right forks, all in the right order, because timing sure is everything.

I was even embraced before dying hair blonde, before trends became mixed, after the slave trade sorted people like bananas into eye-pleasing housemates and those left in the field.

The hair's melatonin is killed, bleached white as ill coral or unwanted stains, the dark energy sapped with Star Wars light like unthreatening beige food, for you have to be just the right amount of other and just the right amount familiar.

Palestine

They were new to the park, at least I'd never seen them before, and my family had lived here for nearly 30 years, I felt I owned the dog park and the village, who were these people with benches dedicated to them, I had never heard of them, who were these people with the muzzled black lab that growled at mine, we were here first, and how ivy-like a feeling that made you walk with cake mix stuck to your heels.

d) ideas on 'little text' (LT)

picked by neither proseposse where older bro got the low-down or pithy class-clowns cutting deep

with equal ratios of fiction and nonfiction, since it's not true that boys into facts and girls, dreams.

I was asked if I valued LT less, if the diminutive expressed a judgement to be read differently.

I gave a mouthful of brambles

saying how interesting we conveyed feelings without being aware, for I hadn't thought,

trying to get LT under the radar subconsciously by giving it another terminology.

Lies

I've only seen one rainbow that didn't pretend to be reachable.
We had indigo poppies last year I didn't paint,
but I know when to draw inaccurately to seem accurate.
I tell you it's your fault because I know it's not,
like we sometimes sing off in our ears to sound right outside,
and when I tell myself I don't need you when maybe I do.

Some see Mol come alive in relationships, like the spark between flint and steel, a relationship to soil and cell can tether and give purpose [go to page 58]

Through thick and thin

On walks we sometimes squeeze through hungry trees of different sizes.

We like thin trees our tongues can wrap and fat trees our arms can't.

Fat men often give good hugs if they have the right temperament.

George II liked fat women it seems, though they weren't fat then.

One of my friends gets fat and thin monthly; another when things wrong,

the rest of the forest spitting acorns at a result of soil, water and weather.

The hammam

flat
like
a
bare
chest
scrubbed
clean
of
its
leaves,
no
rolls
of
note,
riches
awash
like
dirt
aplenty,
marsh
wood
beach
flat-
lands
not
yet
discovered;
she
is
more
than
she
seems.

Playing Sims

1.

I once offered to be an egg donor.
They treated me like an overnight bag
except with pages of forms to fill and
two hour-long interviews even before
I was given such info as having no say
over the child finding me at 18, even
before I knew I was fertile, the eugenics
lab had already asked for my four best
features, my colour and my ethnicity,
even those of my great-grandparents so
that the prospective parents could choose
a version of me like a university campus
or a snack from a vending machine.

2.

My tail twitched and my udders hung
hefty with the unused milk turning to pus
if not what the human race wanted,
so, I'd be butchered and slabbed into
red marble streaks that could have
passed for tuna steaks, the coagulum colour
of old smelly periods, and sold as meat
in local co-operative supermarkets.

The stages of childbirth (or meditations on toxic parenting, by The Depression Project and others)

Pregnancy

In a Catholic nunnery in Ireland, Sean Ross Abbey in County Tipperary, they stole children from mothers and sold them for church profit. Having not had any, I grasped a straw in the haystack, the one not peed on, and imagined my substitute torn from me. I now grasp the neighbouring straw, the one with snot, and drool, and piss, and salt, and laughter spit.

The dense brownie belly of the beerman, compared to the light sponge of fat, interesting through its temporary state; all boundaries are first the mother's, from womb to skin to fluid; no wonder some struggle to respect those of another so dependent on the initial shared driveway, eroding them even when their importance stressed; here, in the navel, is the first sign of toxic parenting.

Birth

This messy business, where juices of all colours and consistencies dampen the soil for growth, the sky for coloured arches, this is where good intentions change into grazes that slowly tattoo a body purple, the colour of fresh bruises before time mellows them into the single malt of tawny and gorse.

This is where critical shifting of the goalposts, like never-ending contractions, can give the impression of perpetual dissatisfaction, success minimisation and control manipulation. This, the dismissal of child preoccupations, buttons pushed even when asked not.

After birth

All that pushing will lead somewhere, to skin tags or urinary retention, maybe unhealthy relationships and low self-esteem, or the seeking of external validation. For the child has learnt love, or like, is conditional,

something to earn, based on what you do not who you are, and interactions with the milk-giver leave drained, worse than at the start, where attachments form far from the placenta.

Crossing the border

I wasn't allowed to tell people my name.
Standing at customs uncomfortable,

as I tried to stop my looks attracting looks,
as I imbibed the now-crusted breast milk

that had once – thirty years ago –
flowed from your memory to mine,

of crossing with furs and golden earrings,
as you knowingly smuggled

your fake identity before we got new ones.
A lifetime of hiding can trickle down

to the riverbed where it lactates
alien creatures, the moving body

of water, like confidence, connection,
a great opener of channels.

e)   Shutup,

like a shop closed for business or a house boarded, maybe the family moved due to a killing that lives with each drive past, stacking up hearsay like a magnetic train, freight piling until you can't see the front, when one day you refer to baby videos of you as her.

---

* *Why does life exist? What makes life feel full, meaningful? What gives purpose? What is the purpose of X where X can be anything from the human species to Edith? Why does X exist? What does X want to live for? [go to page 54]*

The Acclaimed

Queen's Wood in Haringey doesn't belong to the Queen,
Resurrection Bay in Alaska has nothing to do with Jesus,
both could've been called otherwise.

We live as fertiliser, of the mind as much as biological
matter decomposing. Most people are remembered for a
couple of generations, some, a bit longer, a rare few,

as reference terms, for there are too many buds to each
stem a name, a tour leader flag in need to see the crowd
even when relayed round and unsure of first touch,

how many have thought the same or similar
to an acclaimed, and how many acclaimed
have thought differently to that attributed.

---

* Sometimes the same thing must be described in many ways because there is no descriptive word beyond the referential [go to page 30]

A polyptych of experts

*

Your mind a sauna

blood pumping a bouncy castle

feeling somewhere
in the body's scientific name for core

you are hot, cheeks clowned at case
left for a cheese-and-onion sandwich

*

Autistic tests like some other tests last four minutes, are taken on the phone in busy London trafficked streets on stressful lunchtime breaks, slotted in between deadlines like bones in flesh, and consist of answers given by those who have a stake in prognosis, controlled by their desired outcome and sometimes level of need for attention.

*

A doctor once told me it was a shame they often stuck to first diagnoses, digging their heels like a stubborn kid shown wrong, judging that entering book by its cover. He said this at Charité, one of the world's most respected hospitals, in seven minutes where he chose not to look at my back, fingers and legs that wouldn't bend, jotting down on paper his first patient-described diagnosis.

*

Ode to the frigid

or to those who have flying crickets in genitalia that ram their views when the house clutters; not 'chaste' or 'pure', instead such an unloved word, spared the ogling of men but not the heckling, contrary to the purpose of the species, told to coax the 'normal' urges, through increasing sizes of vaginal aids, presented in a pretty box, and this by the doctor – the frigid, who want to get on doing more important things than sweating.

Tinnitus

/ˈtɪnɪtəs/

noun,
MEDICINE

The fire station alarm is constantly on and men shouting at each other Jim's getting the rope Tim the emergency respiratory systems rushing past one another scrambling up and down engines along ladders shiny suits crinkly sheets and hoses longer than gigantic chocolate yules.

How hard the sleepless must try to appear awake,

how those with tinnitus must ignore it, as if their ears have no pig-headed irritants droning in colourful waterpark slides.

Second life

The hot tap is on, music too
and you shut the door with you
on the other side
can you come here please
can you come here please
but none are the reason the doc said
what did you say what did you say
the palms of my valves have worn-out
calluses from aural rock-climbing
when answers punitively not given.

The exoskeleton of the partially deaf

curved with a sturdiness
the millipede or lobster aspire to is
bubble-wrapped from everything,
a walking unbreakable safe
comprising three layers, mostly
calcium carbonate, which might
ring strange if calcium thought soft,
but it muffles all sound, like a
studio vacuum, alienating
and so shatteringly isolating.

---

* Mol is more than Maxim – "No Mol for the universe, reproduction for the human species, subjective for the individual", which, when put like that, makes it seem like magic, that Mol could be in a cupboard in a room but not in a house with the room inside [go to page 14]

Rush hour

confuddles the Professor of Loneliness.
It is harder to make sense of than old age
where friends drop off like war rations.

The crowded traffic of *careerloverent*
makes it tough for the soul
to batter its way on the Bakerloo Line.

Experts say the stoic and suited don't
place importance on the needs of health,
and all lonely people think it's their fault

stuck between growing in a black hole
or falling into it

f)   little philosophy text

Magritte wrote *'Ceci n'est pas une pipe'* next to a drawn pipe (its representation)

This is not a pipe: pipe (its referent)

I write 'this is not a pipe' next to pipe written out (true)

I write 'this is a pipe' next to pipe written out (also true) †

A giant thought the real-world fake, but the idea of a world existed

but ideas are not real or constant, *no referent is just one thing*, x is rarely ever x

Mt Kilimanjaro is rarely ever just Mt Kilimanjaro, x1 is usually x2, x3, x4...

Mt Kilimanjaro is (at some point) the tallest mountain in Africa but not necessarily so † †

Fish roe is a potential, family, food and a grail.

---

† tho philosophers forget visual referent while focussing on sentence sense and truth value referent

† † tho there is necessarily a tallest mountain in Africa if Africa is said to exist

In a world where you can be anything,

be kind, but it's not a world
where you can be anything,
you can't turn into green tea,

although it's funny to think
we'd be aliens if we met aliens,

can't rule without popularity
or money, can't go to the
supermarket naked, or open
all doors with Matilda ease.

It's not true that

pets never disappoint, in the same way it's not true that the sink hole never clogs with hair that shouldn't be there with cutlery and microscopic food; that bird shat on your car and you said it was good luck, the dog shat in the garden and you congratulated it for not going on the path, that human didn't make you feel like shit the one time you were expecting it and you felt forever grateful you'd been let off the hook.

---

* *But Mol is also more than purpose , sense , unsettled by the unknown [go to page 71]*

Things like asparagus

Dragon fruit is like asparagus
so, a Trading Standards court case
or three back-to-back miscarriages in third trimester

positive morning mantras can be
a launch into space
I'm good enough the world fine gonna have a great day

but forgiveness is not asparagus-like
nor pennies that drop, cosmic or other – from theories
of relativity to requests not to wipe hands on bathrobes –

taking longer than three years for that wishing-well miracle

Psalm 15

Murder is a Babybel in wax, from the view of the Universe, where stars burst and planets turn out to be dwarves. Murder is a pineapple or a hedgehog, but for us, the person who took our place in the queue, the Christmas tree star of wrongs. So only after seeing Jason the murderer working in the pub, the psychological abuse he received still not justifying the physical he served, and twenty years after being handed an anger-management leaflet bereaving and leaving dinner: the guilt of a good monster is the hardest to bear, or maybe that of a monstrous good, if such things are even said to exist.

My friend Shane

I wake up and Shane has already plumped the sofa cushions and done the washing up from the night before, the stone worktop sparkles and there's clean space between the now hidden clutter. Everything's pristine thanks to Shane, for Shane wants the house to be prepared for any drop-in, even though the house just sits there and lets Shane busybody around. Shane keeps Shane's mind occupied through Shane's fingers. Shane is clearing out and caching the bits others can't see, because Shane thinks no one would come for tea if they really saw the mess of Shame, because Shame thinks people are quick to judge the mind's biscuit crumbs without finding out why.

S-s-s-

Even the most eloquent can f-fall
game, when time geysers,
space slims,
how it does with fast-moving objects,
cars aside ambulances or fast water
taking more splatter-space than slow

.

In that pending smidge of s-silence,
the stutterer must condense
10 minutes of speech
before end guillotines /

the heart palpitates every millisecond
closer, like with anything dreaded –
a first truth-or-dare kiss, the Monday
start of unloved work, the envelope
on that c-counter

and in that meta-fear   stutterer looks down
embarrassed   ayahuasca awareness   they see
train approaching   them on platform
them   other side
often   unable   leap
caught   /   hope   /
  in closing door.

The juncture

I got to the juncture for the first time alone
teenage me with small firm breasts an older
man would write about

and then I encountered the juncture
numerous times, both sides equally lush or
equally worn – equally unknown
but now I had those breasts men write about
in baggy clothes, making myself less
of a threat to women I wanted to befriend

then in mid-twenties the juncture appeared
again, tho that suggests it hadn't before
            which it had, with every choice,
when excess, speed weed alcohol poppers
even a three-night stand over a two-year
span were tried out

in early thirties, seeing the juncture irritated
so much I thought I wasn't going to be
controlled by it, that I'd surpass it
without traversing it, that I'd sidestep it
altogether, since a career had to be chosen
this late in the game and a lane still didn't
jump out

so I took a helicopter over the juncture
and flew high enough to see the paths of
both tracks, I dropped work/scalp/pesticides
spreading myself thinly like a layer of icing

the thirties quickly went by with simmering
aches and pains, and the juncture appeared
oftener, for even in the air there comes
a point when one lane should tempt
more than another, and I froze, and the
engine stopped, and I fell

the forties came with a greying hair or two,
swollen throat and slightly less allure
tho I still looked pubescent from a distance
people could smell a shrivelling pomelo
and then the juncture appeared once more
harder to spot overgrown with uneven
ground, poor juncture that aged with me

sixty came, seventy came, eighty
juncture still there, juncture angry
"you had all this to give and you
didn't choose, cowardly paralysed
squanderer who never walked
my nakedness stretching out
before you"
"you're right, patient juncture,
downfall of my life, but does it
even matter if we're all going
to be forgotten?"

g)   little recipe

Take my heart; mush it up until you get a thick paste. Don't worry if it hardens, it'll ease later. Keep whisking until stiff peaks form, that rise and jut. Now take the rest of the ingredients and gently fold them into the heart, making sure not to over beat. Each ingredient needs to be distinguishable, separated like a German *trennbares Verb*. In no condition do we want the heart assimilated, its taste floating softly above other flavours, like orange blossom, jasmine or Damascus rose in macaroons. Once you have the mixture, leave it for a few minutes to cool. You should see a slight change in texture and a deflation that is normal. Now turn it upside down, throw it on the floor and jump on it. Keep stamping vigorously until the mixture is completely flattened. Sprinkle a little bit of sugar then twist your feet, sliding from one side of the kitchen to the other. This will make sure that the heart is firmly in all the nooks and crannies and unable to be retrieved. Once you have done this, step back and admire, your mushed heart is now ready to enjoy.

'Mahl' is the German word for 'meal'

There are set ideas about what a meal, or the Meaning of A Happy Life, is or must be, for humans. The world of chairs and crockery, capuchins, might disagree /

sit-down meals needn't be valuable per se / needn't be the goal, there are picnics and barbeques, socialising, chewing and loitering / the quest for true reason can wrongly presuppose an inventor

but I'm not convinced intrinsic value exists, either continuous like a highway, or circular like a roundabout, not unlike John Dewey (an end in a context is a means to an end in another), Monroe Beardsley (nothing has intrinsic value).

The fact we can't pinpoint meaning could reflect the fact we can't pinpoint the end of existence – forever changing, forever relative, forever everything, while time is God.

Foreplay

Cities equal sex
nothing to do
but foreplay
CBD espresso martinis
art of insect labium
preparing you
for friction
or boring to it
with nothing
but nothing synonym.

It puts meaning
into a whole other light.

---

* Can Mol just be a question or the start of, or the continual openness to an experience or experience itself, or life? [go to page 49]

Note on Shakespeare's "Tired with all these, for restful death I cry"

Fatigue calls for standstill (+ what greater stop than death?)

but it's lack of hope that calls for no-return,

the inability to see way out, the incapacity to sustain

a feeling, the accuracy of otherwise self-indulgence

over-the-top, impotence to live this great gift in a desired

way, but even then, we do not cry out, but supplicate

or resign; in fact, you could say despair is the greatest

prayer to life, the greatest prayer to being saved.

Dearest Beethoven,

I too think odes to joys lack on the page
full of unhappiness, all art is about death,
I heard last night, whilst watching a doc,
and I immediately had acid reflux
of the mind. Let's think about the clarity
of the cold sunny sentiment, the hues
of the leaves telling us to get ready for bed
like a mother who knows to depart
the fairground when things good, before
the teacups makes you regurgitate,
candy floss. Age is like that, wearing
until we're more inclined to sleep, though
nothing can prepare you for the narrowing
of everything, nothing can prepare you for
the puddle of piss leaving a stiffening body.

Little dot [hyperventilating in the Universe before finding a modest place]

,   ,   ,
,   ,   ,   ,   ,

, , , , , , ; ; ; ; ; ; ; ; : : : : : : ! ! ! ! ! ! !
@   %   >   % $ >   !   : ---------------

-------------------- . ---------------

...

Dead fox

I saw a dead fox in the road today, in between the coming and going lanes, how a lady of the house would find the sickness of their cleaner an inconvenience. The roadkill had been lustre and bushy-fluffed, with a healthy red glow worthy of taxidermy when I had cycled past fresh in the morning. Now a few hours later, I couldn't look. It had reduced in size like good, boiled sauce, and had crimson tendrils flaying off in Expressionist lines. Mangled and diminished, the forced puberty from girl to woman, an opportunity lost, how through all the chores and chores some don't enjoy the home/life, exhausted when night-time knocks for its ferry fare.

---

* Mol is hidden treasure marked with an X on a disintegrating map. Mol is a bedtime story. Mol is an imaginary friend, the latest fad everyone wants to get their hands on [go to page 18]

A part of my body is dead,

hardened and now so hard you could use it as a door knocker or the beak of a woodpecker; it has turned the soot of Black Death, of Shanghai smog; I want to crack a nut on it like a squirrel, parched walnut brains waiting inside; perhaps it's for the best such rot, or some people, are hard to crack; the dead part of my body is on the extremity, where it's visible unlike emotional death but can't be seen, hidden by socks and shoes like jokes and smiles to ward off the stench of insecurity; it's funny carrying around death like this, death my haemorrhoid, my inherited locket; I live as a different name. They say it's a chilblain gone wrong, stuck too long, but it'll disappear soon too, the way everything does.

ANNEX

Notes: the poems a)-g) can be read as one long sequence. The Japanese gold joining in 'Bread and chocolate' is called *Kintsugi*.

Acknowledgements: Anthony Anaxagorou, Arvon, Raymond Antrobus whose Levels 1-4 writing prompts inspired the title of my poem 'Levels 1 to 4 in 10 minutes' and led to my poem 'Dearest Beethoven,' after Terrance Hayes' 'What it look like', Stuart Bartholomew and everyone at VERVE Poetry Press, Rishi Dastidar, Faber Academy, *Ink sweat and tears* for publishing 'A part of my body is dead,', Jen Hadfield, Wayne Holloway-Smith for guidance and for suggesting Joe Carrick-Varty's poem 'And God said' as a prompt for my poem 'When cortisol rises,', Charles Lang, Jeremy Noel-Tod and *Propel Magazine* for publishing 'Dead fox', Outspoken Press, Poetry School, Claudia Rankine's book *Citizen, an American lyric*, *Tentacular Mag* for publishing a version of 'Playing Sims', Mark Waldron and Maggie Wang. Special thanks to the people I care about, everybody and everything I've learnt from, and the interaction between some form of reality and imagination perceived through a subjective apparatus, which is what I feel a human life experience amounts to. This book is not entirely factual.

ABOUT VERVE POETRY PRESS

Verve Poetry Press is a quite new and already award-winning press that focused initially on meeting a local need in Birmingham - a need for the vibrant poetry scene here in Brum to find a way to present itself to the poetry world via publication. Co-founded by Stuart Bartholomew and Amerah Saleh, it now publishes poets from all corners of the UK - poets that speak to the city's varied and energetic qualities and will contribute to its many poetic stories.

Added to this is a colourful pamphlet series, many featuring poets who have performed at our sister festival - and a poetry show series which captures the magic of longer poetry performance pieces by festival alumni such as Polarbear, Matt Abbott and Genevieve Carver.

The press has been voted Most Innovative Publisher at the Saboteur Awards, and has won the Publisher's Award for Poetry Pamphlets at the Michael Marks Awards.

Like the festival, we strive to think about poetry in inclusive ways and embrace the multiplicity of approaches towards this glorious art.

www.vervepoetrypress.com
@VervePoetryPres
mail@vervepoetrypress.com